Hangin' With
THE
BACKSTREET
BOYS

Hangin' With

THE BACKSTREET BOYS

by Michael-Anne Johns

An Unauthorized Biography

SCHOLASTIC INC.
New York Toronto London Auckland Sydney
Mexico City New Delhi Hong Kong

Photo credits/front cover: Edie Baskin/Outline

ISBN 0-439-04532-0

12 11 10 9 8 7 6 5 4 3 2 1   8 9/9 0 1 2 3/0

Printed in the U.S.A.

First Scholastic printing, September 1998

To my nieces Desiree, Dominique, Jessica, and Sarah, and my nephew Kevin Jr. — my own Florida sunshine stars.

Contents

Hangin' With
THE
BACKSTREET
BOYS

1
Backstreet Boys: In the Beginning!

"We've been together every day for four years now. . . . It's like family. I never had a little brother, but now I've got four."
— *Kevin Richardson* (USA Today)

California has Hollywood, full of glamour and glitz. Illinois has Chicago, known as the Windy City. New York has Manhattan, the city that *never* sleeps.

It could go on and on and on, but this geography lesson ends in Orlando, Florida — home of Disney World, Universal Studios, and now the BACKSTREET BOYS!

Twenty-year-old A.J. McLean, twenty-five-year-old Howie Dorough, eighteen-year-old Nick Carter, twenty-three-year-old Brian Littrell, and twenty-six-year-old Kevin Richardson are the Backstreet Boys. Although they formed their group in Orlando, they have conquered the record charts all over the world — in Europe, Asia, Australia, South America, and Canada. Now they are back home conquering America. But back in Orlando in 1993, if you had told the five boys what the next five years would hold for them, well, they probably would have asked you if you were selling a psychic hotline!

Orlando Magic

But let's not get ahead of ourselves. Actually the Backstreet Boys story begins with record producer Louis J. Pearlman. A cousin of Art Garfunkel — half of one of the 1960s most popular and influential groups, Simon and Garfunkel — Lou Pearlman had grown up loving everything about music. Of course by the 1980s, Orlando was fast becoming a magnet for young performers who hoped they could get a job at one of the theme parks and eventually be "discovered." And Lou was on the lookout to discover a talent that he could help develop.

Meanwhile, in 1992, a twenty-year-old Kevin Richardson was pursuing his dream of a singing career in his hometown of Lexington, Kentucky. He was performing with local pop groups, singing cover songs of Top 40 hits. But Kevin quickly got bored with that routine. So, on a whim, he decided to move to Orlando, Florida, to see if he could make that next step to fulfilling his dream. Within a week of moving to Orlando,

Kevin landed a job as a Disney World tour guide. When Kevin wasn't showing tourists around the parks, he appeared in park parades and events as the character Aladdin, and one of the Teenage Mutant Ninja Turtles. But he hadn't given up his dream of being a singer/songwriter.

One day, Kevin and a Disney World co-worker were on a break, talking about what they wanted to do with the rest of their lives. Kevin revealed he wanted to hook up with a singing group again, and his friend suggested he meet "these three guys who harmonize all the time."

The three harmonizers were A.J. McLean and Howie Dorough, who were in high school at the time, and Nick Carter, who was in junior high. They were local boys who had met at various acting and singing auditions and performances. They became friends and formed a singing group in the style of their favorite groups Boyz II Men and Color Me Badd. When Kevin first heard their *a cappella* (without musical accompaniment) harmonies and saw their dance-floor maneuvers, he knew he had found a home. A.J., Howie, and Nick welcomed Kevin enthusiastically, but they decided they needed one more voice to finish the group. Under the guidance of Lou Pearlman, who had seen the boys at several talent shows, they held auditions, and tracked down leads all over Orlando. But when they still hadn't found the right voice to complement their sound, Kevin had a bright idea. He made a quick long-distance call back home to Lexington, Kentucky. It was early in the morning and a school day, but Kevin couldn't wait — he just had to talk to his cousin Brian Littrell. As a matter of fact, Kevin called Brian's school and had him pulled out of class! Almost without taking a breath, Kevin told Brian about the group he had just joined and invited him to come to Orlando to check it out! The very next day Brian headed to the airport and took off for Orlando . . . and eventual superstardom!

One Day at a Time

From the beginning, the five guys could feel something click as their voices blended in song. But knowing you're good and breaking into the music industry are two different things. They decided to take things one day at a time. The first thing they had to do was choose a name for the group.

They knocked around a bunch of different names, but then they came up with "Backstreet." Howie explained to *SuperTeen* magazine: "It was actually a flea market, the Backstreet Market in Orlando. It was like a hangout place."

"We had to name it something," Nick adds, "and we knew we wanted to add 'Boys' at the end of it — kind of like the Beach Boys. So Backstreet Boys was just a name that we collectively decided on."

The next step was a bit harder. It was making the connection with someone who was already hooked into the music business. That's where Louis J. Pearlman really started the ball rolling. When he first heard A.J., Howie, Nick, Brian, and Kevin harmonize, Lou knew he was in the presence of musical magic! So Lou (who Brian renamed "Big Poppa," and later thanked on their first album notes with, "If it wasn't for your dreams, our dreams wouldn't be possible"), brought the boys to music managers Donna and Johnny Wright. This married couple had a company called Wright Stuff Management and they had already had quite a successful run in the pop music world. Johnny had been the road manager for the New Kids on the Block at the height of their popularity, so he knew the ups and downs and the ins and outs of the business. Donna traveled with Johnny and was his right-hand person. Lou just knew they were the right choice to help guide the Backstreet Boys' career.

At first Johnny was a bit hesitant to take on a five-boy pop group. "Before I saw them perform, I wasn't sure if we wanted to get involved," he told *Billboard* magazine. "The New Kids had just finished up two years prior. But hearing them sing just gave me chills running from the back of my heels to the top of my head. I really felt like we had something there."

BSB Hits the Road

The Wrights began setting up gigs for the Backstreet Boys at schools and the area theme parks. Kevin told *Billboard* that those early performances really opened the Boys' eyes to how important it was to perfect their act. "Those were the hardest crowds to perform to. You could tell they were thinking, 'What is this, the second coming of the New Kids on the Block?' But once we started singing *a cappella* and showing them we could really sing, we won them over every time."

The Wrights often used these performances as audition showcases for record label executives on the lookout for new talent. But Johnny and Donna didn't just wait around for the talent scouts to find them. "We'd go to local labels and sing *a cappella* in their foyers," Brian remembers. "We'd sing anywhere, for anybody."

And if a label A&R (artist and repertoire) executive didn't arrive at a show on time, Donna pushed the speed dial on her ever-present cellular phone and got him to listen anyway! She would hold up the phone so the executive could hear the Backstreet Boys perform, as well as the crowd's enthusiastic reaction.

Soon the Backstreet Boys had become a local

phenomenon and they were performing all over Orlando — from high school events to opening for Brandy to concerts at Orlando's theme parks. Then the grassroots word spread and the Backstreet Boys were being offered gigs all over Florida and even out of state.

"We auditioned for like five or six different labels," recalled A.J. at a press conference in Los Angeles during a video shoot. "Then, the one label that chose us, wasn't even there! We were in a middle school, in a gym. This was before we were even really known. We just came running in wearing our own clothes, not even wearing wardrobe. It looked like your bunch of average kids running in right off the street. We went over huge."

At that school gig in Cleveland, Ohio, Donna did her old "hold up the phone" trick for David McPherson of Jive Records, and he caught the magic! "We got signed right after that," Brian says.

The Big Break

Barry Weiss, the president of Jive Records (U.S.) was very excited about signing the Backstreet Boys. "When we heard the way these five guys [could] sing, we felt that they are as real for the pop genre as Garth Brooks is to country and our own R. Kelly is to the R & B market. . . . We see this group, because of their vocal ability, as not being just a teen-appeal group, despite the fact that [teens] are going to be a very big part of their audience. . . . It's not, like we said, 'Oh, my God, there's a void in the marketplace for teen groups. Let's go out and sign one.' When we signed this group, it wasn't too dissimilar to when we sign any other group. We believe that there is real artistry in what they do," Weiss told *Billboard* magazine.

Once they were signed, Nick, Howie, A.J., Kevin, and Brian headed into the studio and began working with producers Veit Renn and Tim Allen. In 1995 they completed the single "We've Got It Goin' On," and it was released both in the United States and in Europe. Everyone in the Backstreet Boys/Jive family impatiently awaited the weekly chart reports — only to be disappointed. "We've Got It Goin' On" only went to number 69 on *Billboard*'s top-pop chart.

As for the seeming disinterest in the U.S., Howie reasoned, "The scene wasn't exactly right for our style of group. Grunge was still heavily going, rap was really hard, and the pop scene wasn't really in phase at the time."

The funny thing was that "We've Got It Goin' On" was causing a stir in England, and then throughout the rest of Europe. It amazed some industry experts, but Brian observed, "Over there they had a bunch of what's called 'boy groups,' so we had a ready-made market. But since we were American, we were a fresh new sound for Europe. We had more of an edge, and unlike a lot of those other boy groups, we were more than just a bunch of pretty guys. We could sing."

And then there was Johnny Wright. He couldn't help thinking back to the late 1980s when New Kids on the Block released their very first album. It was a disaster in the U.S. It practically only got airplay in Europe, and it wasn't until the New Kids' second album that they became major stars in America.

So Johnny Wright began looking across the Atlantic . . . and saw gold and platinum!

2
World Conquerors

"Backstreet Boys only sing live and do five-piece harmony, a cappella. . . . We just want to make everyone realize that we are real, there's nothing fake. . . ."
— *A.J. McLean* (Reuters)

Even without a full album recorded, Johnny and Donna decided to make an "American Invasion" of Europe with the Backstreet Boys. BSB had only three singles by the time they started touring over there: the up-tempo dance track "We've Got It Goin' On," which was produced by Denniz Pop in Sweden and would eventually be the first cut on their debut album; the romantic ballad "I'll Never Break Your Heart," which was recorded back home in Orlando; and the thoughtful "Roll With It," which was cut in a Chicago recording studio.

The Backstreet Boys stage show included

these three songs and covers of some of their favorite songs by singers who had influenced them, such as Elton John, Luther Vandross, and Michael Jackson. They toured as the opening act for the group PJ and Duncan, and very soon BSB was causing a buzz on the circuit. While "We've Got It Goin' On" didn't break them huge, "I'll Never Break Your Heart" certainly did. As a matter of fact, in December of 1995, they won the *Smash Hits* magazine "Best New Tour Act" award — a major honor in the British music world. Then they performed the song, which had gone gold (sold 500,000 copies), on England's number one music TV show, *Top of the Pops*.

England and Beyond

The Backstreet Boys' conquering march spread quickly over the rest of Europe. In January of 1996, "I'll Never Break Your Heart" went gold in Germany and they were voted "Number One International Group" by viewers of that country's TV network, VIVA. Later that same month, BSB crossed back over the Atlantic, but this time they landed in Montreal, Canada. They were doing a small promotional tour to support the release of "We've Got It Goin' On," and at a shopping mall appearance in Montreal they got a taste of what the future held for them. Nick, Howie, A.J., Brian, and Kevin only had a short set planned for the appearance, but so many girls crowded in to see and hear this new singing sensation, things got crazy. Fans were so excited that thirty-five girls collapsed during BSB's performance — and Johnny Wright was recalling the New Kids on the Block hysteria!

By February of 1996, the Backstreet Boys were selling out shows throughout Europe and Canada — and they still hadn't even released an album yet! "We've Got It Goin' On" was added to Montreal's Musique Plus Television's (the French-Canadian equivalent of MTV) regular rotation list, and for the next twenty-six weeks they were the station's Video Battle Champions! At a radio station appearance in Hamburg, Germany, BSB drew such a huge crowd of fans that the police had to surround them and escort them to their waiting cars.

"We've been at radio stations in Germany and had to climb out of the windows to get out of the place," Nick told Steve Jones of *USA Today* about the European reaction to BSB. "But in the end, it's all fun. We sit and laugh about it."

A.J. also recalled another appearance at a Berlin radio station. "The girls were outside this building," he told *Teen Machine* magazine. "We thought some kind of club was going on, but apparently it was a bunch of fans waiting for us. We went upstairs to do our thing on the radio station and we got pinned inside. They were blocking the stairway and the exits. Our security got us out but warned us not to sign autographs. Well, dummy me, decided to sign an autograph while Howie's being yanked away — Howie's yelling and I'm not noticing, just standing there happy and signing autographs!"

The crowds seemed to double at each and every BSB appearance and when they released their debut album, *Backstreet Boys*, in Europe and Canada in April 1996, the records stores couldn't keep it on their shelves!

The Seed Was Planted in U.S. Soil

The irony was that American fans couldn't go to their local record store and pick up this CD — it wasn't released in the U.S.! However, savvy teen magazine editors in the U.S. sensed these five Orlando-based boys could fill the pop music void left when New Kids on the Block became NKOTB and then broke up.

Hedy End, editorial director of *SuperTeen* and *Superstars*, was the first to start covering Backstreet Boys in her magazines. It was a bold step to take because it was difficult for her readers to find copies of the Backstreet Boys singles or CD. But soon other editors of magazines such as *BOP!, Tiger Beat, Teen Beat,* and *16* were in total agreement with Hedy and were running cover stories and pull-out pinups on BSB, too.

Meanwhile, the Boys were continuing their

world takeover. During the summer of 1996, they worked nonstop as the headliners in a totally sold-out, standing-room-only, fifty-seven-date European tour. Along the way, they were getting reports that "We've Got It Goin' On" and "Get Down" were earning gold and platinum (selling one million copies) status in country after country after country. In August 1996 they won Germany's prestigious VIVA Comet Award as "Best Newcomer." When they returned to Montreal to perform for 70,000 screaming fans at an outdoor festival, they learned their "Get Down" video had knocked out "We've Got It Goin' On" as Musique Plus Television's Video Battle Champion.

In the fall of 1996, BSB continued their global march and brought the fever to Korea, Hong Kong, Japan, Malaysia, New Zealand, and Australia. Then it was back to Europe for a second tour that included England, Germany, Norway, Austria, Sweden, and France. The final honor in Europe during 1996 was when BSB was nominated — along with multi-platinum acts Oasis, Jamiroquai, Boyzone, and Spice Girls — for the MTV Europe Viewers' Choice Award. BSB was the *only* American act nominated in the category — and they won!

BSB finished up 1996 with the official Canadian release of the *Backstreet Boys* CD and saw it go double platinum within two weeks and eventually six-times platinum. A thirty-two-show Canadian tour that featured the songs from the CD, *Backstreet Boys,* was sold out twenty minutes after the tickets went on sale!

"It was some kind of year," Kevin observed.

Johnny and Donna Wright agreed . . . and knew they had just accomplished the first part of the "BSB Big Picture." The next would be the homecoming!

3
Backstreet in the U.S.A.

"We finally have time to focus on our homeland. We got our start everywhere else, all over the world, except home, so it's time to just come back, relax a little bit, and focus on the U.S. fans."
— *Brian Littrell* (UPI)

Nick, Howie, A.J., Brian, and Kevin were happy to be back home in Orlando in early 1997. After all, they had been on the road almost nonstop for the previous year and a half. But their homecoming wasn't going to be a vacation. Oh, no! The boys went right into the recording studio, working on new songs, rearranging old ones, and even learning the producing end of making an album. They were getting ready for their major assault on the American market and they wanted to give it their all.

"We've always wanted to bring it back home,"

Nick explained. "We wanted to make sure we brought it back strong."

Kevin agreed with Nick; he told *Tiger Beat* magazine, "We want to bring it home. We want our teachers, and family, and friends to see what we've been doing with our lives."

In a press conference interview with several teen magazine editors, Howie explained his take on their delayed homefront attack: "This is our home country and we've been waiting so long to come home. We took the backwards approach, going around the world and then coming back here. But I think, looking [back] on it all, it was a good decision. We wouldn't change anything because we got the chance to really hone our craft and got a chance to see the world. I think a lot of artists who become big over here, then go around the world — they just go briefly, in and out, just for the show. We got the chance to actually go into these countries and actually see the culture, visit some of the really small cities. The people there really appreciated us."

And in another teen magazine press conference, A.J. and Brian added their thoughts on the subject. "I think the second time is a charm for us instead of the third time," A.J. observed. "I think we are going to be more legit this time. Better music."

Brian added, "I'm very excited, I'm very happy,

yet I'm very nervous because you never know what the future holds and we've worked so very hard all over the world to come back here. Who knows?"

The Work Begins

So the conquering of America was well thought out. But the BSB family knew it wasn't necessarily going to be easy. Hedy End of *Super-Teen* and *Superstars* recognized the hurdles the Backstreet Boys had to overcome back in the U.S. Shortly before they released their single "Quit Playing Games (With My Heart)," she commented in a *USA Today* interview, "They've got their work cut out for them. They have to reintroduce themselves to a national audience and to radio, and wait and see what happens. But certainly they have a nice buzz coming from overseas."

In another interview, this time with *Billboard*, Hedy End explained why the music scene had been somewhat barren territory for the teen magazines for a while. "There have been a lot of older celebrities in the charts. There was also a lot of [hardcore] rap music that didn't necessarily appeal to our readers. It's a little too serious and often didn't have very nice things to say about girls and women, so there was no real interest from our readers."

But times, they were a-changin'! Groups like

Hanson and musicians like Jonny Lang proved to the record labels that young artists could draw huge audiences — as long as they were real, as long as they weren't "created" just to be a teeny-bop sensation. Ike, Taylor, and Zac Hanson can sing and play instruments — and write their own songs. Sixteen-year-old Jonny Lang brought the blues to a whole new audience. And those who had first recognized the talent and appeal of the Backstreet Boys several years before, were betting that an American teen audience with newfound respect would too. They were right!

The Cheers Begin

The debut American CD, *Backstreet Boys*, had an August 12, 1997 release date. It included some of the songs that were on their overseas releases *Backstreet Boys* and *Backstreet's Back*. The first single from the CD — "Quit Playing Games (With My Heart)" — hit the radio stations on June 27. It debuted on *Billboard*'s "Hot 100 Singles" chart its first week as the Hot Shot Debut at number 24. Within two weeks it climbed to the number 2 spot and soon topped the charts.

And why did it work this time? Perhaps it's because the Backstreet Boys were not just a put-together pop group, they were the *real* thing and though their solid fan base may be with teens, their music appealed to *everyone*. A.J. told a *Teen Beat* reporter on the set of the video shoot for "As Long As You Love Me," "I think [it's] the versatility of the album. We cover every ground of every age group of every race. We don't just specifically want to cover one type of people. We want everyone to love our music. That is what Backstreet Boys is all about. Family, fun, and stuff like that."

Of course, Jive Records wasn't going to overlook the fans who had been impatiently waiting to finally get a taste of their homeboys — the American teens. Jive let out all the stops. They attached 65,000 BSB sampler cassettes to the "Love Stories" book series, mailed samplers directly to subscribers of the "Sweet Valley High" book series, included samplers in the JCPenney's Kaboodles makeup cases, distributed samplers at summer cheerleader camps, and made BSB videos and CDs available to be played — nonstop — in the junior departments of a number of chain stores.

Jive marketing executive Janet Kleinbaum explained a two-pronged strategy to *Billboard*, "The band's influence is not limited to the teen market, but you have to build from a base, and we know that these young fans are particularly active. They are the ones that are going to rush out to make the scene. Besides, I don't think adults are going to know that there is a teen market for this band because they're not reading *Teen* magazine. They are seeing the band's videos and hearing them on [Top 40 radio stations.]"

There were a lot of industry types who agreed with the BSB advisors. *People* magazine's Backstreet Boys review read in part, "They may be getting harder to tell apart, but all male vocal groups are not created equal. While many in the R & B camp convey soulfulness by moaning, groaning, and contorting their voices in mock pain, their more pop-conscious counterparts in Backstreet Boys sing like they're having a ball. Already international megastars, with more than eleven million albums sold outside the U.S., the Orlando-based quintet has struck gold at home with the Top 5 single 'Quit Playing Games (With My Heart).' Their [self]-titled debut CD fares best when the funk flows, but ballads like 'Quit Playing Games . . .' and 'All I Have to Give' are so peppy, despite a tinge of melancholy in the group's harmonies, one can't help smiling. . . ."

Seventeen magazine advised in a special going-to-college section of their August 1997 issue, "First rule of college: Study hard. Real hard. Rule number two: Get funky! Get loose! Get it goin' on with music that's got it goin' on! Jive Records' Backstreet Boys are five very fine guys who sing *a cappella*. Heavily influenced by groups like All-4-One, Boyz II Men, Shai, and Jodeci, BSB's album is an R & B romantic's delight. Powerful ballads speak straight to the yearning heart and outrageous live harmonies make any heart swell. Check 'em out . . . on Jive Records."

And in Fred Bronson's June 28, 1997, "Chart Beat" column in *Billboard*, he observed that the Backstreet Boys' success might play turnaround and open the door for some new European boy groups! "Groups like Boyzone, 911, OTT, Worlds Apart, and Arvingarna have not made the same inroads domestically that they've made on the continent," he wrote. "So it could be considered a breakthrough for the genre to have the Orlando, Florida-based Backstreet Boys take Hot Shot Debut honors with their finely crafted pop single 'Quit Playing Games (With My Heart).'"

Double Duty

Striking while the iron was hot, BSB not only released their first American CD, but in 1997 they also released their second Canadian/European CD, *Backstreet's Back*.

Shortly before the release of *Backstreet Boys* Kevin explained to a *Teen Beat* reporter how the songs were selected. "This album has five of our singles that we released in Europe already. Great songs. Since we released our album in Europe, lots of producers became interested in working with us and we have gotten some really great new songs added. So, it's like the best of what we've been doing for the past two years. We are really excited."

At the time of that interview BSB was busy making back-to-back videos for all their markets. Over the summer, they went to Los Angeles for some studio work and filmed the videos for "As Long As You Love Me," "All I Have to Give," and, for their European market, "Backstreet's Back."

Not only were they busy, but they knew they had achieved a certain status when they got respected director Nigel Dick to work with them on the "As Long As You Love Me" video.

"We are getting a little more clout, a little more say in who the director [of our video] is," A.J. told a *Teen Beat* reporter. "Nigel Dick is a wonderful, wonderful director. He is so creative and he works with us. He doesn't boss us around, saying, 'You do that, you do that.' He's like, 'What do you think if we do this? What do you think, fellows? Does this make you uncomfortable?' He cares about our well-being and he is looking through our eyes, [seeing] how we want ourselves to look. It's great. And we are getting ready to do another video next week . . . which will be a Nineties version of Michael Jackson's

Thriller video concept. It's all done in a kind of dream sequence and there are lots of twists."

A.J. was obviously enthusiastic about the horror-style video for "Backstreet's Back," which is the first single off their European CD of the same name. He told *BIG!* that the concept was a group effort. "All of us thought of it. We had the idea that our bus breaks down and we have to go to a castle, where Brian falls asleep . . . he's dreaming and he turns into a werewolf. . . . It's definitely a step above the normal Backstreet Boys video."

Howie jumped in and told the British magazine reporter he loved the morphing scenes where they turned into monsters. "I really wanted to get some of those cats'-eye contact lenses, but they have to be specially made and there wasn't enough time. I did have my own set of porcelain fangs though. They made them from the same material they use for dentures."

And in a nonstop gab-fest with *Teen Beat* and *All-Stars* the five boys couldn't say enough about this unique video. When asked how they came up with their characters, Howie explained, "We all chose our own. I was Dracula, Nicky was a mummy."

Kevin jumped in with, "They wanted me to be Frankenstein —" Nick interrupted with, "He would have been a great Frankenstein . . ." Then A.J. added his two cents with, ". . . Just because everyone knows that character, but when they finished him with the makeup and long hair and nails, his character came out cool."

Taking a Breath!

As 1997 was coming to an end, Nick, Howie, A.J., Brian, and Kevin needed to take a little time just to chill. But first they had one more major commitment: the Macy's Thanksgiving Day Parade!

On November 27, the Backstreet Boys bundled up in blue and black reversible down jackets to protect themselves against the twenty-to-thirty mile-an-hour winds that were blowing down the parade route. It was so windy that there was even a moment when the parade bigwigs considered "grounding" the famous character balloons. Instead, they flew them low so they wouldn't be caught up by the gusts of wind.

But no wind was going to stop the Backstreet Boys. Nick, Howie, A.J., Kevin, and Brian climbed aboard "The Future From Here" float sponsored by Fuji Photo Film USA. And as they sang "As Long As You Love Me," the Hip Hop Kidz were dancing on the float and the fans, who had waited for hours to see BSB, cheered and cheered!

As they waved to fans, they were getting ready to return to Orlando to take a month off to relax. But according to Kevin, the day after Christmas, the rush was to start again. "We go to Canada," he told a Scholastic magazines writer. "We have a show up in Halifax, Nova Scotia, then we're going to do five shows in Montreal and the Sky Dome in Toronto."

And that's not all. They are working on songs for their second American CD and their third Canadian/European release. "We hardly ever have spare time, but when we do, the record company manages to get us in the recording studio," laughed Howie to a *Teen Beat* reporter. "We're always thinking ahead to the next album, or the next video — what we can do better, be more creative, go to another level," added Kevin. "And with the writing, too — especially the third album. We're going to collaborate with Denniz Pop [and] Full Force. So we're real excited about the writing because we've learned a lot in the past couple of years from the writers and producers we've worked with, and eventually we want to be writing and producing our own stuff."

New Year's Resolutions

Well, it seems that Nick, Howie, Kevin, A.J., and Brian got all the wishes they ever had. But that didn't mean they were going to let down their enthusiasm or energy. If anything, 1998 would have them running even harder.

BSB wants to keep their fans happy and bring in lots of new fans, too. Says Nick of the future, "We hope to have just as many fans [in America] as around the world. At the same time, we're not going to leave our [international] fans in the gutter — [they] were there for us in the beginning. The plans we have right now are just to basically be ourselves."

4
Busy Boys

"I think one thing that's really cool is, American fans pay attention. They study you. And in a way it's very cool, because you know they're paying attention to what you sound like."
— Nick Carter (16 magazine)

The year 1998 has the boys running even harder than before! Concerts. Benefits. TV appearances, and more!

On the Tube

During the month of February, the Boys continued their conquest of the U.S. via television. In case you missed 'em, here's a quick rundown of when and where they were seen: *ABC in Concert* (February 6), *Ricki Lake Show* (February 13), *Nickelodeon's All That* (February 14), and *Sabrina the Teenage Witch* (February 15).

Live from New York, it was the Backstreet Boys on *Saturday Night Live* on March 14. Their sizzling performance rocked the audience, and all the viewers who tuned in!

The Boys Give a Little

On Sunday, March 15, 1998, Florida got a whole lot hotter when the Backstreet Boys pulled into town for a concert. Together with 'N Sync, Lyte Funkie Ones, Solid Harmonie, 95 South, Vanilla Ice, and twelve other Orlando-based bands, the Backstreet Boys helped raise money for the victims of 1998's devastating tornadoes. The concert was held for almost 9,000 screaming people in the parking lot of the Hard Rock Café at Universal Studios, under a blazing sun for nearly four hours.

Besides raising money from the concert tickets, silent auctions were held and raffle tickets were sold. And the grand prize for the raffle was a lunch date with Howie Dorough!

The raffle raised about $2,000, but what went on during the silent auction, as reported on the Backstreet Boys' official Web site, was pretty wild! One of the silent auction items was another lunch date with Howie, and by the end of the day, the highest bid was for $5,500. Just as the number was written down, another woman grabbed the clipboard and wrote down $5,501! Then, the woman who wrote down $5,500, took the clipboard and tapped the second woman over the head with it! But don't worry — it didn't end in a brawl! *Both* women agreed to have lunch with Howie for a grand total of $12,000!

Video Debut

The Backstreet Boys debuted their first U.S. home music video on June 2. In this cool *All Access* video, Nick, A.J., Brian, Kevin, and Howie invite you to join them for an insider's chance to see what really goes on at a Backstreet Boys' video shoot. The video also contains personal interviews with each member of the group, previously unreleased concert footage from around the world, and some of the group's favorite music videos: *Quit Playing Games (With My Heart), As Long As You Love Me* and *Everybody (Backstreet's Back)*.

BSB on Tour

The Backstreet Boys kicked off their world tour on July 8 in Charlotte, North Carolina. Here's a look at their tour schedule as of press time:

DATE	LOCATION
July 8, 1998	Charlotte, NC
July 9, 1998	Jacksonville, FL
July 10, 1998	Miami, FL

July 11, 1998	Orlando, FL
July 12, 1998	Atlanta, GA
July 15, 1998	Blistrow, VA
July 16, 1998	Philadelphia, PA
July 17, 1998	New York, NY
July 18, 1998	New Haven, CT
July 19, 1998	Albany, NY
July 21, 1998	Darien Lake, NY
July 22, 1998	Cleveland, OH
July 23, 1998	Fishers, IN
July 24, 1998	Detroit, MI
July 25, 1998	Louisville, KY
July 26, 1998	St. Louis, MO
July 28, 1998	Houston, TX
July 29, 1998	Dallas, TX
July 31, 1998	Kansas City, KS
August 1, 1998	Chicago, IL
August 2, 1998	Milwaukee, WI
August 4, 1998	Denver, CO
August 6, 1998	Salt Lake City, UT
August 7, 1998	Las Vegas, NV
August 8, 1998	Los Angeles, CA
August 11, 1998	San Francisco, CA
August 13, 1998	Portland, OR
August 15, 1998	Vancouver, BC, Canada
August 17, 1998	Calgary, Alberta, Canada
August 18, 1998	Edmonton, Alberta, Canada
August 19, 1998	Saskatoon, Saskatchewan, Canada

August 20, 1998	Winnipeg, Manitoba, Canada
August 22, 1998	Toronto, Ontario, Canada
August 23, 1998	Montreal, Quebec, Canada
August 25, 1998	Halifax, Nova Scotia, Canada
August 27, 1998	Hempstead, NY
August 28, 1998	Scranton, PA
August 29, 1998	East Rutherford, NJ
August 31, 1998	Grand Essex, VT
September 1, 1998	Providence, RI
December 1, 1998	Köln, Germany
December 2, 1998	Münster, Germany
December 3, 1998	Berlin, Germany
December 4, 1998	Leipzig, Germany
December 5, 1998	Kassel, Germany
December 6, 1998	Mannheim, Germany
December 7, 1998	Zurich, Switzerland
December 9, 1998	Friedrichshafen, Germany
December 10, 1998	Weis, Germany
December 11, 1998	München, Germany
December 14, 1998	Hamburg, Germany
December 15, 1998	Frankfurt, Germany
December 16, 1998	Stuttgart, Germany
December 17, 1998	Bremen, Germany
December 18, 1998	Kiel, Germany
December 19, 1998	Essen, Germany
December 20, 1998	Köln, Germany

5
BSB One by One

"Considering we're with each other 24–7, we've
grown to love each other. We have a tight bond. We
know which buttons to push
and which not to."
— *Howie Dorough* (USA Today)

Nick Carter — Naughty and Nice!

Nick's parents, Bob and Jane Carter, always
maintained that their blond-haired, blue-eyed
baby boy was a "firecracker" from the day he
was born on January 28, 1980 — in the same
Jamestown, New York, hospital as legendary
comedienne Lucille (*I Love Lucy*) Ball!

Even as a toddler, "Little Nicky" was a born
entertainer. His family gladly tells tales of their
baby boy, clad only in diapers, bustin' a move on
the dance floor of the family club. "It was a
lounge called the Yankee Rebel, which my fa-

ther and Grandfather both owned — it was a small place," Nick recalled in an interview with *SuperTeen*. "We had a little dance floor at the Yankee Rebel, and my dad used to be a DJ and play records. When I was real small, I used to get up there in my diapers and dance around. I have pictures of me with headphones on that were bigger than my face. I was just a little chunk; everybody used to call me Charlie Brown."

At any rate, the Carters knew very early on that Nick loved to perform, loved to make people smile and clap as he sang and danced. Soon, a new addition to the Carter family was clapping along with Nick's "fans." That was sister B.J., who was born when Nick was two. Those times in the warm and loving country home on Webber Road held happy memories for Nick, but when he was almost six years old, his parents decided to move down to Florida and start a new business.

"They packed up their old Cadillac El Dorado and loaded all our stuff into a little trailer," Nick continued in his *SuperTeen* interview. "So we made it to [Tampa] Florida and we moved into our first house. It was a retirement home — that's where my dad started working. We lived there for maybe a year. It was [big enough] for sixteen people, but we built on to it."

When Nick was about seven, the show biz bug

bit and he even remembers entertaining the residents at his parents' retirement home. "I'd come in and sing for them," he told *Live & Kicking* magazine. It was kind of sad 'cause I had a few favorite [residents] there, but they soon passed away."

As Nick was performing to larger and larger audiences, his family was growing by leaps and bounds, too. His sister, Lesley, and fraternal twins, Aaron and Angel, were born down in Florida.

In the fourth grade, Nick landed the lead in a production of *Phantom of the Opera*. He entered a lot of talent shows and recalls one in which he tried an impersonation of Elvis — leg shake and all! "I had to try," he told *Live & Kicking*. "I'm not really a dancer though. I was always so nervous doing those things. You gotta remember, I was really young when I started doing that stuff."

But he was doing something right and was soon the featured vocalist at the Tampa Bay Buccaneer pre-game shows. This NFL gig lasted two years, and then when Nick was twelve, he won the 1992 *New Original Amateur Hour* TV show. Local commercial gigs came quickly after that — Floridians may remember little Nick promoting the Money Store and the Florida State Lottery.

Nick kept himself busy performing and auditioning at local Tampa and Orlando events, and though he was only in junior high, he made friends with two older guys he kept running into at the same gigs — A.J. McLean and Howie Dorough. The three started passing the long waits at auditions and performances by harmonizing together. They started kicking around the idea of forming a group, and when Nick was offered what many would consider the chance of a lifetime, a gig at Disney World, he had to make a decision. It was easy. Nick said no thanks to Mickey and Minnie and yes to working with A.J. and Howie. And that was the birth of the Backstreet Boys!

But what about Nick off stage? Who's his best friend? What are some of his favorite childhood memories? Just ask him — he'll be glad to tell you all about it.

When the Carter family moved to Tampa, Nick made a whole new group of friends, but when he was about eleven or twelve years old, he became best buds with a boy named Brent. "We used to always hang out together," Nick told a Scholastic magazines writer. "We used to get in trouble all the time — not bad trouble! There was this big pond where we lived — we used to go fishing there. And I remember one time Brent and I sneaked into this shed that was there and took some shovels out. We started digging in the lawns and everything, and we left [the shovels] there and just took off! We were bad!"

Of course, Nick grew out of that mischievous stage, and after his love of performing, he developed an interest in water sports, especially scuba diving. "I've been a scuba diver since I was twelve," he told *16* magazine. "When I was fifteen I got my open water permit — that's a regular diving license. Before that I had a junior permit that allowed me to only go seventy-five feet deep. With an open water permit there are no restrictions. . . . My dad is a diving instructor, so he was always with me when I went deep. With an open permit, you can go wreck diving, night diving, and deep [sea] diving."

When Nick turned seventeen, he also got a boat. "I keep it berthed on the canal next to my house that leads to the Florida coast," he revealed in an online interview. "I fill the engine with gas and just head out to the sea. The Florida Keys are the greatest stretch of ocean in the world with lots of small islands you can stop off at. Many a time, I've played football on the beach with my brothers and sisters. A lot of times I go out on the boat alone. Being on my own, with just the silence of the sea, is such an escape from the constant screaming of fans on a Backstreet Boys tour. It's something I need to do — just to get away from it all. To me, the Florida Keys is paradise on earth!"

A.J. McLean — He's Not Dopey Anymore!

"'I'm a big ham and I gotta be out there and doing crazy stuff for no apparent reason, especially on stage!'" admits A.J. But then one might have guessed that there was something brewing when, as a youngster in his very first acting job, A.J. brought the house down as Dopey in *Snow White and the Seven Dwarfs.* . . ."

That's how A.J.'s Jive Records biography begins, but A.J., who was born on January 9, 1978, loves embellishing on that first moment in McLean stage history. He even told a Scholastic magazines writer that it was his best childhood memory! "It was my first performance. I started in musical theater and it was my first role. It's kind of funny. They weren't sure I was a good speaker. I grew up with a speech impediment. I had a lisp and I stutter — I still do. I guess I think slower than my mouth speaks, but my first role was in a show called *Snow White*. I was Dopey. He didn't say anything. He was a little mute. I was about seven. Basically, for lack of a better word, I stole the show. I was the main squeeze. All the girls thought I was really cute. And I went out and signed autographs for all the little kids. And it was funny — back then I signed my full name, because that's what I thought you were supposed to do. But now, I just write 'A.J.' because that's who I am. But back

THE
BACKSTREET
BOYS

A.J., Howie, Kevin, Brian, and Nick

Paul Bergen/Redferns/Retna

Back in the beginning of BSB, November 1994.

Janet Macoska

In Cleveland, Ohio — shortly after they were signed by Jive Records.

Janet Macoska

The Boys at the 1996 MTV Europe Music
Awards, where they won the Viewers' Choice Award.

AWARDS 1996

Joe Major/London Features

At the press conference launching their
U.S. debut album in New York City.

Meet the Boys.....

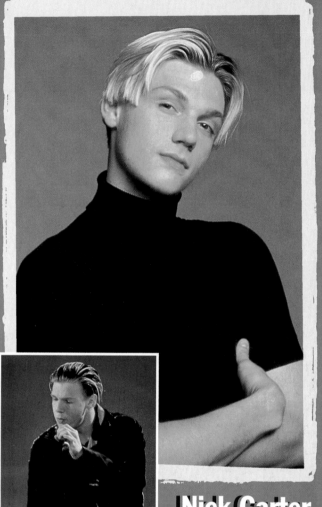

Paul Bergen/Redferns/Retna

Larry Busacca/Retna

Nick Carter

Marko Shark/Corbis

Kevin
Richardson

Eddie Malluk

A.J. McLean

Brian Littrell

Howie Dorough

The Backstreet Boys meet the press.

Ernie Paniccioli/Retna

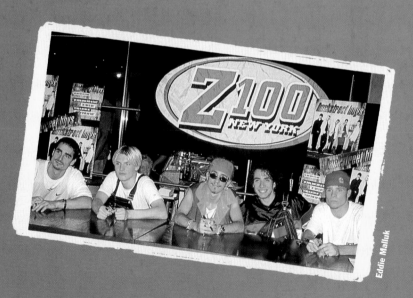

Eddie Malluk

The Boys are always willing to lend a hand. . . .

In Cleveland the guys pitched in with the community cleanup and then performed an *a cappella* concert for the volunteers at a local service project, "Christmas in April."

They took part in Nickelodeon's "The Big Help" to promote volunteering in Los Angeles.

At the central Florida relief benefit "Orlando Bands Together," Kevin fills out a check donation for the tornado victims of central Florida.

The guys share a laugh while performing at "Orlando Bands Together."

The Boys captivate
their fans . . .

Larry Busacca/Retna

whether they are singing ballads . . .

Eddie Malluk

or funky R & B.

Aaron takes after his big bro Nick—he's got his blond hair *and* his singing talent.

BSB: Without a doubt, they're here to stay!

then I wrote 'Alexander James McLean.' It would take me forever!"

By the time A.J. was in sixth grade, he had appeared in twenty-seven productions, including *The Nutcracker*, *The King and I*, and *Fiddler on the Roof*. When A.J.'s family moved from West Palm Beach, Florida, to Kissimmee, which is right outside of Orlando, his show biz bug had really bitten! While he was in junior high, he won a part on Nickelodeon's *Hi Honey, I'm Home*, and he also took on some Disney channel projects. During that time, A.J. took numerous classes in dancing, singing, and acting — he knew what he wanted to do. Of course, it all clicked when he met up with Nick and Howie.

But what about those nonBackstreet Boys times for A.J.? You might be surprised to know he loves to read the classics and poetry. Books of literary greats such as Shakespeare, T.S. Eliot and Edgar Allan Poe fill his own personal library. He also likes to write poetry, so it's not surprising that A.J. is very interested in song writing. "I like to sit by the pool and write music," he told *BOP!*, "and sometimes if I have the opportunity, I'll go to our manager Johnny Wright's house and record my own ideas."

He might do something else with his poetry, too — at least that's what he told a reporter for *Teen Beat* and *All-Stars* when she asked if he thought about publishing them as a book.

"Maybe," A.J. said. "I've written about seventy-five poems between when I was about fifteen and now. If I ever get the real time to sit down and go back over them, spell-check them, proof-read them, and maybe make a couple of changes, maybe I will."

Most of A.J.'s fans know he is very close to his mom, Denise. As a matter of fact, many of them have probably seen her and don't even know it! "I started traveling with the group with A.J. as his guardian because he started when he was under eighteen," Denise told a *Teen Beat* and *All-Stars* reporter at the "As Long As You Love Me" video shoot. "I'm not the type to sit around, so I started helping him with wardrobe and makeup. I had done theater work, so I knew how to do that. So I styled him for photo shoots and things in the beginning. [I did] everything from selling T-shirts to getting him dressed, to selling cassettes, to doing everything on the road. I eventually got into wardrobe, and started doing that for [all] of them."

Does it ever cause A.J. "problems" having his mom on the road with him? "No, we have a good time actually," Denise laughs. "[It's been just] he and I together most of his life, so [we're] buddies."

Of course, like any mom, there are times Denise gets a little concerned about her son. "You know, typical things, like going out real

40

late when he knows he has to get up for something in the morning," she admits. "Or eating
the wrong foods and not taking care of himself.
That's about it."

Well, Denise's influence seems to have worked
some magic, because A.J. recently told *BOP!* he
was making a concerted effort to change his
ways! "I'm going to try to chill out on the
McDonald's food," he said. "Sometimes I eat too
much of it and I've had problems in the past
with my stomach. I don't want to make it worse
than it is, so I'm trying to eat less greasy, fatten-
ing foods, and take better care of myself."

Howie Dorough — From "Baby Face" to BSB!

When Howie was only three years old (he was
born on August 22, 1973), he jumped onto his
grandmother's bed and sang her the old classic
song, "Baby Face." Part of the Dorough family
legend includes those times little Howie would
jump up on a bed and start singing and playing
his little guitar!

Back then Howie was a major Michael Jackson fan. "Michael had a big influence on my life,
in terms of inspiring me to sing," Howie told
BOP! "He's a great artist. He's incredibly tal-
ented. When I was a little kid, I had the album
Thriller, I had the Michael Jackson glove, and I
even had the *Thriller* skateboard!"

However, there was a point in Howie's early life when he was thinking about another career! "I had an uncle who was a doctor and my father was actually a police officer," Howie revealed in an online interview. "So it was between those two [careers]. But once my sister got me involved at the age of six or seven [in theater], then I started dreaming that someday I would be singing live in front of a big audience."

"I really started performing when I was seven," Howie told *16* magazine. "My first play was *The Wizard of Oz* — I played a Munchkin." But that was just the beginning. Quickly Howie got into the fast-track show biz whirl. He performed in Orlando community theater productions such as *The Sound of Music*, *Showboat*, and *Camelot*; he did a Nickelodeon pilot called *Welcome Freshman*, appeared in the films *Parenthood* and *Cop and a Half*, and "did tons of commercials for Walt Disney World." And, in his spare time, he sang in his church choir!

Howie knew that show biz was going to be his life and he even earned an Associate of Arts degree in music. No wonder many consider him the backbone of BSB. He's always looking ahead to the future. But Howie doesn't forget those who have been there all along the way. Especially the original grassroots Backstreet Boys fans. "I'd just like to tell them, thanks for all the support," he told a *Teen Beat* reporter. "We've been gone for a while and I want to thank them for constantly supporting us. Now we're back home and now we're ready to take on America and hopefully we can have the same support and keep the BSB pride alive!"

Kevin Richardson — Farm Boy to Backstreet Boy!

Kevin is definitely a real country boy. Born on October 3, 1972, he spent the first nine years of his life on a ten-acre farm in Harrisburg, Kentucky. And when his family left the farm, they moved into a real modern-day log cabin on the grounds of a summer camp/retreat. "My father managed the summer camp and retreat center," Kevin told a *Teen Beat* reporter. "It was a church camp. I was fortunate to grow up there and I had tons of friends, because every summer the camp was full of kids my age and older and younger. I just kind of had all kinds of friends. I met people from all over the state, and sometimes from all over the country as well."

In his Jive Records bio, the oldest of the Backstreet Boys states, "I had a great childhood. I loved school, played Little League football, rode horses and dirt bikes, and sang into a hairbrush in front of my bedroom mirror."

Kevin got his first set of keyboards when he was a high school freshman, and one of the first things he did was join the chorus and drama club. As a matter of fact, Kevin claims there were two high school teachers who particularly influenced him. "First there was my drama teacher, Ms. Betler," he told a Scholastic magazines writer. "And also my geometry teacher, Mr. Lutes. They were characters themselves. They were good — they made [learning] interesting, fun, and creative. Mr. Lutes was a minister, so he was a very good public speaker who had a way with words. He could really get your attention in class."

Well, Kevin learned about getting attention! And he loved every minute of it. "When you're on stage, you can see people's reactions and that is the greatest feeling of all," he told *All-Stars* magazine. "That's why we're here. That's the natural high."

When Kevin isn't performing, he likes to just be as normal as possible. "I like to hit the gym first, then go and hang out in a mall and look around, buy some CDs, maybe go look at some clothes. . . ." he told *BOP!* "Then I like to take a nap and probably watch some TV — just relax."

Of course, if the reaction to the Backstreet Boys is any indication — Kevin won't be doing much relaxing for quite a while!

Brian Littrell — The Comedian

According to Howie, Brian is definitely the group funnyman! "He keeps us laughing," says

44

Howie. The funny thing is that Brian's first exposure to music and performing was anything but on the light side. Born on February 20, 1975, he spent his early years in Lexington, Kentucky, singing at his local church, other regional churches, revivals, and even weddings.

What many don't know is that Brian feels he has a lot to thank God for. You see as a young child he was very ill and didn't even know it. "I was born with a heart murmur," he told *BOP!* "I have a hole in my heart. I lived the first five years of my life with this hole in my heart and the doctors didn't know."

It wasn't until a day back in 1980 when he was playing around his Lexington, Kentucky, home with his older brother Harold, that his parents found out their little boy was seriously ill! The boys were roughhousing and Brian fell and cracked his head on a sidewalk. His parents took him right to the Good Samaritan Hospital — and then complications set in. He got a blood infection. Brian explained, "I had no chance of living whatsoever. The doctors were telling my mother and father to go ahead and make the funeral arrangements."

But then the unexpected happened — even while the doctors were predicting the worst, Brian surprised everyone and recovered completely!

"I had a great childhood," Brian said in an online interview. "Since I didn't become a Backstreet Boy before I was eighteen years old, I had time to graduate from high school. If I hadn't gone for music, I'd probably have gone to college."

But singing did enter his life and Brian made a beeline for it. Though he is the first to admit there were times he hit a speed bump or two. Like the time he let his comic side take over his singing side. "I was in the play *Grease* in high school," he told a Scholastic magazines writer. "I was one of the greasers. I wasn't the main one — I was Roger. And I was one of the T-Birds. . . . There was a scene where [I] get my pants pulled off on stage and show my boxers. . . . It was kind of dorky, but I thought it would be cool and outrageous for the high school play. I'll never forget it — I've got a big, long video and I enjoy watching it every so often!"

When Brian got his cousin Kevin's call about the audition for the Backstreet Boys, he knew it was right. And when he met A.J., Howie, and Nick, he felt right at home. Being a part of BSB gave him a chance to do something he'd wanted to do ever since he was five years old and recovered from his near-fatal illness. "I think that's why God gave me the gift to sing," he told *BOP!* "So I can bless other people's lives."

May 1998 brought some big changes in Brian's life, when it was announced that he would have to undergo heart surgery. But fans breathed a big sigh of relief when Brian came through the surgery just fine. Brian requested that instead of cards and flowers, his well-wishers send donations to the Brian Littrell Fund for Pediatric Cardiology at St. Joseph Hospital in Lexington, Kentucky. Brian planned to rejoin the Boys on tour as soon as he recovered.

6
Backstreet Baby: Aaron Carter

"I wanted to be a singer mostly because I wanted to see Nick all the time."
— *Aaron Carter* (Teen People)

There's a new kid on the block — ten-year-old Aaron Carter, the adorable little brother of Nick Carter. While big brother Nick's been touring with the Backstreet Boys, Aaron's been wowing audiences overseas. Aaron actually formed a band when he was seven, but soon decided to go solo. He currently has two huge hits overseas, "Crush on You" and "Crazy Little Party Girl," and released a single in the U.S. in June. And tons of fans got to check out Aaron in person when he opened for the Backstreet Boys on their 40-city tour that began in the summer of '98.

Aaron has also filmed four videos. The first, *Crush on You*, was filmed in Los Angeles with bro Nick. Video number two, *Crazy Little Party Girl*, was filmed in Vancouver, BC, Canada. And numbers three and four, *I'm Gonna Miss You Forever* and *Shake It,* were filmed in Florida.

Even though Aaron's music is a little more like rock than Nick's, the brothers still have a lot in common. In fact, if you look at a picture of Nick from a few years back, and a picture of Aaron today, you can see the resemblance.

For those of you who are not familiar with Aaron, or who want more info on him, here's the scoop:

Full Name: Aaron Charles Carter

Nickname: A.C. — BSB gave it to him in Germany!

Birth Date: December 7, 1987 (he has a twin sister Angel!)

Birthplace: Tampa, Florida

Home: A house in Ruskin, Florida

Pets: Cats Sugar, Bandit, Lucky; Dogs Simba, Salty, Pepper, Samson

Fave Singers: Backstreet Boys, 'N Sync, Tom Petty & the Heartbreakers

Fave Sport: Football

Fave Food: Pizza

7
Girls! Girls! Girls! . . . Go BSB Crazy!

"I drove into my apartment complex, and [the fans] know my car because a picture of it had been in a magazine. And these two girls — one was from Germany and one was from Switzerland — were sitting right in front of my apartment with their pens and paper, and they jumped up as soon as they saw me."
— *Brian Littrell* (USA Today)

They are probably five of the cutest boys in the world. Definitely five of the most popular! But all of them — Brian, Nick, A.J., Kevin, and Howie — will tell you that being part of the Backstreet Boys doesn't automatically mean you'll have a girlfriend. At least not a relationship they would really like.

On the subject of girlfriends, Nick told a *Teen Beat* and *All-Stars* reporter, "It doesn't work, it doesn't work that good. If you think about it, in our situation — if we were just here in the United States, maybe it would work. But, man, we are everywhere: Asia, Europe, Canada, everywhere. We're always gone for like months at a time."

To a *SuperTeen* reporter, Nick further explained, "We meet a lot of girls, but we're never in one place long enough for relationships to develop. I'd feel sorry for us if we did have relationships. It's very hard when you're always on the run."

Picking up where Nick left off, Brian once opened up his heart during an online interview and explained one of the reasons why he hasn't settled down. "[A relationship] is something you really miss when you tour as much as we do," he said. "Everybody wants to be loved and have a special friend. But I'm not a guy who fools around, I don't want to hurt anybody, and, of course, I don't want to get hurt myself. Right now it wouldn't work for me to have a steady girlfriend since we'd never get the chance to meet each other. I think all five of us in the group have tried to have relationships. I had a girlfriend in the beginning, but it didn't work out. I know that many people in this business exploit their fans, but I would never dream of doing that."

Actually, A.J. tried to test the on-the-road relationship principle a couple of years ago and he found out the hard way it just doesn't work. "I had my heart broken," he told *TV Hits*. "When I broke up with my last girlfriend, I felt horrible! We had been going out for more than three years and I was madly in love with her. [When we broke up] I was down for weeks, nobody could even talk to me."

Okay, so you get the picture: the Backstreet Boys *don't* have girlfriends right now. But that doesn't mean they aren't looking!

A.J. told *BOP!* he's first attracted to a girl's eyes. "Honestly. I know that most guys would not agree with me, but the first thing that I look at . . . is eyes. I have to look into her eyes because if I could look deep past those eyes, it's like 'Wow!'"

Brian is one of those guys who *does* agree with A.J., and he revealed to *BOP!* that after making eye contact, he likes to get to know a girl who has a "great personality and [someone who is] very open and trustworthy and giving and just willing to have fun."

As for Howie, well he confessed to *TV Hits* that his ideal girl would be Cindy Crawford, but that he ". . . couldn't imagine her as my girlfriend. I like more natural-looking girls. I'm into girls I can talk to for hours without getting bored. My dream girl has to have a great sense of humor. Girls who don't talk at all aren't very attractive, but she shouldn't be Miss Chatterbox either! . . . It's great if a girl is confident and accepts herself. . . . She's got to be intelligent and shouldn't be afraid to speak straight from her heart. Confidence is very important. I've got to be able to trust my girlfriend and be able to talk to her."

In the same *TV Hits* interview, Kevin confessed that looks are not all that important to him when it comes to being attracted to a girl. "The most important thing is that we can talk on the same level," he said. "She's got to be intelligent and confident about what she's saying. I don't like people who lie or break promises."

And then there's Nick. A while back he was quoted as saying he only liked brunettes — and boy did he get in hot water with all his blond, redhead, and even multicolored hair fans! Ever since then, Nick has realized he should never limit himself to things such as hair color. "I like long hair, it doesn't matter what color," he told *TV Hits*. (Oh, no, what about short-haired girls, Nick?!!!) "More than anything her personality counts. A girl who always agrees to everything is not for me. I love a challenge, the risk that things could go wrong! . . . [But, I'm faithful], very! That's important to me. I could never date a girl who was going out with another guy, and I could never see any girls besides my girlfriend. I would feel bad and I wouldn't be able to look her in the eye anymore. If I had a girlfriend, I'd never even look at other girls."

But for Nick and the others, that seems to be in the future. Right now, they are trying to keep everything in perspective. After all, everywhere they go, there are girls, girls, girls. "It's very flattering, that's for sure," Howie admitted to *Tiger Beat*. And A.J. added, "What guy wouldn't want girls screaming over him? I keep thinking, I'm just out of high school, I'm just a regular guy, why are you crying?"

But for now, Nick, Brian, Howie, Kevin, and A.J. don't want girls crying over them — unless it's because they are moved by one of their songs! For now, the girls they meet and get to know become friends, good friends. "I've got a lot of close girl friends," A.J. told *BIG!* "In fact, I've got more girl friends than boys who are friends. I get along cool with guys, but they're more into that sport/male thing. I am too, but I'm also into shopping, buying clothes, and stuff."

One thing all the guys really like to do is surprise the friends they have made all around the world with phone calls when they least expect it. You never know, if you're lucky enough to meet the Backstreet Boys during their travels, your phone might be ringing, too!

8
BSB on the Hot Seat! They Answer Your Most-Asked Questions

"No matter what happens, if any of us go off, we're always going to come back together.
The Backstreet Boys' name will always be there, no matter what."
— Nick Carter (BB magazine)

What makes you cry? What makes you laugh? How did you meet? Nick, Howie, A.J., Brian, and Kevin are always bombarded with queries from reporters, fans, and even friends wherever they go. Check out their heartwarming and funny answers to the questions they are most often asked!

What's the most expensive thing you've ever bought?

Nick: "Probably a gold chain that cost about three hundred dollars," he told *Smash Hits* back in 1996. "I bought it for myself." However, things have changed since that interview. In 1997 Nick got his driver's license and bought his dream vehicle. "A deep forest green 1500 Chevy step-side truck," he told a *Teen Beat* reporter. "I'm thinking about lowering it, dropping it, getting it all phat."

How often do you shave?

Nick: "That's a weird question," Nick laughed when the *Smash Hits* reporter asked this question. "I just shave a small amount, about once a week, I don't need to shave any more than that, really."

What was your most embarrassing moment?

A.J.: "I embarrassed myself when we did a photo shoot where I was dressed as The Riddler in this green spandex outfit," he confessed to *Smash Hits*. "I mean, I looked like Jim Carrey! Anyway, I went out on stage and introduced our two opening acts dressed like that. The audience went absolutely nuts and all the guys were tripping out — they were, like, 'I can't believe you did it!'"

Nick: "We play jokes on each other," Nick told *SuperTeen*. "One time on stage, I found myself singing into a banana! They stuck it on my microphone." Another time, Nick told *BIG!*, "We did a number, I danced too wild and was going to do a certain move we practiced. My pants were a bit too big and they were held up by my boxers. So when we landed from the jump, my pants fell down! Swoosh! The whole audience got to see [my boxers] and they screamed, of course."

Brian: "Once we were performing a song from the new album on stage and I had to sing the first two verses," he told *Live & Kicking*. "The dance routine was really difficult and I was concentrating so hard on it that I blanked on the words. I ended up just humming along. The others were useless. They were [cracking] up laughing and didn't try to help me out at all!"

What's your idea of a good night at home?

A.J.: "Sitting in front of a log fire with hot chocolate and marshmallows and some mellow music playing," he told *BIG!* during a BSB interview. "It'd be great if the moon was shining in, the lights were low, and it was cold outside."

Nick: "I'd be at my parents' home. I'd get in loads of food and play computer [games] all night with my brother and sisters."

Brian: "I'd have one of those huge movie projectors in a big snugly room with a huge soft couch and beanbag [chairs] all over the floor. I'd make dinner downstairs with the lady of my choice, then we'd go upstairs and watch a movie." Here is another of Brian's favorite ways to spend an evening: "If I'm home, I'll meet my three best friends and we'll go to the [movies]. We always meet a crowd of people we know . . . We have loads of popcorn 'cause I love it. Then we'll head off for a meal. I love steaks, fries, and salad. Then we'll all go back to my house and watch videos and chill out. We get to bed about two A.M."

Do your parents treat you special because you're a Backstreet Boy?
Nick: "No way!" he told *Teen Beat.* "When I go home, I still do chores. If I gotta take out the garbage, I gotta take it out!"

What's your worst habit?
A.J.: "I borrow clothes and toiletries and everything from the guys," he confessed to *Live & Kicking.* "Then I keep them so long that by the time they get around to asking for them back, I've worn or used them so much, they don't want them back anymore. It's a great trick!"

Do you read your fan mail?
Kevin: "Obviously we can't read every letter," he told a reporter at a 1996 Montreal's Musique

Plus Television event. "We've set up fan clubs to help us. Usually we pick fans in different countries to help set up and organize the fan clubs. They help us answer all the mail we get."

What were you like as a child?
Nick: "When I was a young child, I wasn't a very social person. I tried to stay focused," he told Scholastic magazines. "I wasn't one of the popular people in school. I was very unpopular. Other kids were more mature than me in a way. . . . Maybe it was the other way around, since I was around grown-ups all the time. Though I liked school, I had to leave it because I was acting and singing. [My classmates] didn't understand why I left, and they were jealous in a way."

How often do you need a hug?
Kevin: "I could use a hug every day, but I'm not likely to get it," he told *BIG!* during a BSB chat. "It's something I really miss."
A.J.: "As often as I can get one! For me, it's even better than a kiss."
Howie: "I love hugs and kisses. I think it's because I grew up in a big family. Even now I grab my mother and give her kisses all over her cheeks and she's like, 'Oh, Howard, pleeeease!'"

What's the sweetest thing a girl's done for you?

Kevin: "Probably the coolest thing was when I was really sick and this girl I was dating rang her mother to get a recipe for chicken noodle soup, and she made it for me from scratch," he told a *BIG!* reporter. "Isn't that sweet?"

What has surprised you most about being in the recording industry?

Nick: "The biggest surprise for me was walking into a store and seeing our single on a shelf," he revealed in a *Teen Beat* interview. "I couldn't believe it — it was sitting next to all these artists!"

Brian: "It's a lot of work!"

Kevin: "The whole process of how the recording industry and the radio stations and the record companies work, as far as production in the studio. I've been soaking it all in. It's been a great experience and we've learned so much."

What's the best show biz advice you've gotten?

Kevin: "We sang for the Temptations backstage when they were doing a show in Orlando," he recalled in an UPI report. "[A member of the Temptations told us], 'The music business is two words — music and business — and while you're on stage performing your music, you gotta have somebody watching your back to make sure your business isn't walking out the door."

A.J.: "At an awards show, right before going on stage, Robbie Williams [former Take That member] said to us, 'Let me tell you guys a little something: Be true to yourself, never lose sight of what you have, and be aware that it can be gone tomorrow. You never know when it could be over.'"

Nick: "Bryan Adams told us we should keep going in the same way we are and not change just because other people tell us to," Nick revealed in a *BIG!* article. "He said the most important thing in life is doing what you believe in yourself. Bryan was young when he started, so he should know."

Do any of the Backstreet Boys have a secret?

A.J.: "I'd like to do a movie with either Geena Davis or Dustin Hoffman," he told *Teen Beat*. "And to [play] a bad guy. I would love to be the villain, because everybody seems to love the villain more! I mean, the good guys win, but the villains are the ones everyone likes."

If you had three wishes what would they be?

Brian: "I would wish for lifelong health for me and my family, success in life, and a beautiful wife and family," he told a Musique Plus reporter when they appeared in Canada.

Howie: "Since we've traveled all around the world and seen many countries and new faces and new places, I would wish for world peace, seeing everyone live life to the fullest, no hunger, no poverty. That would definitely be my first wish. My second would be to be able to have my family with me everywhere in life. And my third [would be] just to be successful with the Backstreet Boys and us to continue the rest of our lives together."

Kevin: "A long, long, happy career in the music business because I love music and without music I don't know what I'd do. I'd like to have a nice family, so I'd wish for a nice wife and family someday. And, uh, just health, good health."

A.J.: "I wish I could own McDonald's [laughs]. No — I wish for the knowledge to press on and be as successful as I can with these four guys, till death do us part. I wish for a long, long life of health with my family, to support my family and make sure that they can have their dreams fulfilled, as well as mine. And to keep on doing what I do best and to never quit."

Nick: "I wish we could have great success with this group, just like the other guys said. I wish I had a long life. And last, but not least, I'd like to say [that] we've been all around the world and we've seen things from bad to good, and I just wish for world peace."

What's your first memory?
Nick: "Most of my good memories are since I moved to Florida," he told *Live & Kicking*. "But I do remember falling out of a tree when I was living in upstate New York. I was really, really young, and hiding from my sister B.J., who was playing on the swing. I lost balance, fell and hit my head on the bottom of the tree. I cried real bad!"

What's the most important thing your parents have taught you?
Howie: "To be honest, to be truthful to myself and to the people out there," Howie revealed in an online chat. "And that there's nothing we can't accomplish in this lifetime, that we should just go for our dreams."

When you're on the road do you share hotel rooms?
Howie: "We used to — until we started pulling each other's hair out," he laughingly told a *SuperTeen* reporter in June 1997 when BSB was in Los Angeles to film the video for "As Long As You Love Me." "No, we've gotten to the point that we've made a little bit of money, so now we can finally afford our own rooms. It's good. We're

with each other 24–7, so we sometimes need just a little bit of time just for ourselves."

What's the hardest thing about being on the road?

Brian: "It's being away from home and not having a girlfriend," he told *BIG!* "We don't get time to meet girls, chat with them, and then go out on a date. It takes me a while to get to know a girl, so it's really hard. Our schedule is so busy that I can't find time to date!

Nick: "I miss my brother and sisters," Nick told *BOP!*

Kevin: "I like trying foods from different places," he told *Smash Hits*. "But after a while I miss some good American food."

A.J.: "You'll be in one city in the U.S., and you have to fly to Spain for one day," he told a *Teen Beat* reporter. "You don't get enough sleep."

Howie: "You get jet lag a lot," he told *Teen Beat*. "Sometimes, when you finally catch up, you take off again, so your body never gets balanced."

Why do you think you made it big in Europe before America?

Howie: "America just wasn't ready for us," he told *USA Today*. "Rap and Hootie and the Blowfish were really big. We decided to take advantage of Europe. America is the final frontier. It's our home country and it's very important. We took a backward approach. This is the cake. All the rest is icing."

Brian: "It's a bit easier in Europe," he told a press conference. "[In Europe] there is a more mixed taste in music." And to a Scholastic magazines writer he explained, "Breaking in in the U.S. has a lot to do with timing. When we first released 'We Got It Goin' On' in September of 1995, which was over two years ago, the music scene was very alternative. . . . When we came out, pop music wasn't really very strong. There was also a lot of heavy R & B and rap — Snoop Doggy Dog and Dr. Dre. Now you have the Spice Girls and Hanson — it does open a lot of doors for the music scene to come back around. 'Quit Playing Games (With My Heart)' was our fourth single off our European album and it was our first number one hit. . . . I think a lot of success comes from keeping things simple. 'Quit Playing Games (With My Heart)' is so simple to sing along to, it's a radio-loved song!"

Kevin: "I think the fact that it happened everywhere else first was good for us," he told a Scholastic magazines writer. "I think it prepared us a little for what it was like to be in the limelight, and do interviews and TV shows. I think it helped us grow a lot, and I think it improved what we do. I'm actually glad it happened overseas first."

Do you have a group ritual before you go on stage?

Brian: "We have a group prayer — we all join hands and have a prayer," he told *Teen Beat*. "It's more or less a focusing point, with us saying, mentally, what we have to go out there and accomplish, what we have to do. We pray for safety, that no one in the audience gets hurt or falls, because when you're dealing with a lot of people, sometimes it gets out of hand."

A.J.: "We usually sit and eat dinner together and talk about all the important details," he said at a press conference. "Then [we] change together and put on a little powder, if it's necessary to hide a small flaw. About an hour before we go on stage, we warm up our voices and bodies. There was this one time, when we didn't have time to warm up first, and after the show, we were really sore. So that's very important. But the most important thing is our 'group pray.' We don't go on stage unless we've done it. . . . We thank God for giving us yet another day, and for [allowing] us to do what we so desire."

Kevin: "We do a lot of *a cappella* singing together and warm up about thirty minutes before we go on stage."

Who's the biggest scaredy-cat of the group?

Howie: "People always jump on me and I'm like

'Ahhhh.' I'm always jumpy, but not so much that I'm scared of the dark," he told *BIG!* magazine. "Brian's scared of heights so he doesn't like going on roller coaster rides — but he's no scaredy-cat."

Nick: "I'm always scared on planes," he told *Live & Kicking*. "I hate flying. I think I get better the more often I fly though. None of the others get scared, but they don't try to help. They just ignore me."

Brian: "Nick is scared of the dark!" he told *TV Hits*. "If we've been to see a scary movie or something, and we're sharing a room, if the lights are off when we walk in, he's like [whispering] 'It's dark in here, isn't it?' And he's not being funny or anything. He means it!"

Is there anything you always bring on the road with you?

Kevin: "I always bring pictures of my family," Kevin told a *Teen Beat* reporter. "My father, my mother, my brothers, and my god baby. I don't really bring any good luck charms, not really."

A.J.: "I used to bring my blanket — the blanket I had for fourteen years! I went to a hotel in North Carolina and I think the maid thought it was a rag — because it looked like a rag — and threw it away!"

9
Stacks of Stats and Facts!

"We want a future like the Eagles, the Beatles, or the Beach Boys. New Edition made a big impression on us: They were successful young, and they lasted."
— *Howie Dorough* (USA Today)

NICHOLAS GENE CARTER
Nicknames: Chaos, Nicky
Birth Date: January 28, 1980
Zodiac Sign: Aquarius
Birth Place: Jamestown, NY
Current Residence: Tampa, FL
Weight: 160 pounds
Height: 6'
Shoe Size: 11
Hair: Blond
Eyes: Blue
Parents: Bob and Jane Carter

Siblings: Bobbie Jean (B.J.), Lesley, and twins
Aaron and Angel

Heritage: "I am Blackfoot Indian and I might
have a bit of Spanish blood in me," Nick told
BOP!

Pets: Cats — a Persian named Muffy, a Siamese
named Blue Boy, and a mixed cat named Bandit. (Bandit and Muffy are "Hemingway"
cats — direct descendants of cats that lived at
the legendary writer Ernest Hemingway's
Key West home. Because the cats were so in-
bred, they developed a distinctive quality —
each paw had six toes. Muffy and Bandit have
that "Hemingway" mark!)

Dogs — A Doberman named Conrad and a
golden retreiver named Simba; he used to
have a Scottish terrier named Boo Boo, but he
died in an accident in 1996

First Ambition: To be a singer

Musical Instruments: Drums, guitar

BSB Group Position: Lead vocals

School: Adams Junior High, before he started
home schooling

FAVORITES

Music: Alternative

Singer: Steve Perry

Musical Groups: Boyz II Men, Nirvana, Journey,
Wu Tang Clan

Song: The Cure's "I Will Always Love You"

Backstreet Boys' Song: "Quit Playing Games (With My Heart)"

Movies: *Braveheart* and any of the *Alien* movies

Actors: Jeff Goldblum, Bruce Willis

Actresses: Sigourney Weaver, Helen Hunt, Sharon Stone, Christina Ricci

Supermodels: Claudia Schiffer and Cindy Crawford

TV Shows: *The X-Files, Mad About You,* reruns of *Married . . . With Children*

Food: Extra-cheese pizza

Breakfast: Frosted Flakes, toast with peanut butter

Snack: Twix

Chewing Gum: Big League Chew — "it's the purple kind"

Ice Cream: Mint chocolate chip and chocolate-chip cookie dough

Drinks: Coca-Cola, Orange Gatorade, bottled water

Color: Green

Cars: Camaro and Corvette Stingray

Clothes: Nike

Cologne: Gravity

Deodorant: Speed Stick

School Subjects: Science, history, English, physical education (least favorite — math)

Sports: Water sports like scuba diving (Nick has

an "open water license," which means he can go into deep water); football, horseback riding, basketball, baseball

Sports Teams: Tampa Bay Buccaneers for football; Florida Marlins for baseball

Video Games: Alien Trilogy, Mortal Kombat Trilogy, Super Mario — Nick recalls the first time he played a video game. It was in his family's Jamestown, New York lounge, the Yankee Rebel, and little toddler Nick had wandered off. When his parents started looking for him, they found him at the Pac-Man machine. "I had pulled up a stool," Nick told *SuperTeen*. "There I was in my white diaper, sitting on the stool playing the game. That was where my love for video games began!"

Pastimes: Video games, drawing, fishing

Place: The Florida Keys

Holiday: Halloween

Saying: "It's all good!"

UP-CLOSE-AND-PERSONAL

Innie or Outtie (bellybutton): Innie

Dream Girl: "Everyone wants a girl with a perfect personality. It doesn't matter how they look."

Dream Date: Scuba diving in the Florida Keys

First Time on Stage: "I was nine years old and going to Miles Elementary school. I did my first play — *Phantom of the Opera.* They needed a good singer to play Raoul and I had been taking singing lessons."

First Album He Ever Bought: A Journey album

Commercials: The Florida State Lottery, Sears, The Money Store

Little Known Fact: Nick had a very small — "almost an extra" — role in the hit Johnny Depp movie, *Edward Scissorhands*

Collections: Football cards

Most Prized Possession in His Bedroom: "My Michael Jordan pictures."

Worst Part of Touring: "I hate flying!"

What He Wears to Bed: T-shirt and boxers

What He Brings on the Road: "My Nintendo 64 or my Play Station."

Who He Would Like to Ask Out for Dinner: Christina Ricci — "She's fine!"

Most Embarrassing Moment: When the other guys threw him out of the dressing room in front of a bunch of girls. The problem was, Nick was dressed only in his underwear!

Known As: The group's practical joker!

ALEXANDER JAMES McLEAN

Nicknames: A.J., Bone, Mr. Cool

Birth Date: January 9, 1978

Zodiac Sign: Capricorn

Birth Place: West Palm Beach, FL

Current Residence: Kissimmee, FL

Hair: Brown
Eyes: Brown
Weight: 130 pounds
Height: 5'9"
Parents: Denise and Bob McLean (his parents were divorced when he was four years old)
Siblings: None
Grandparents: Ursula and Adolph Fernandez
Heritage: Spanish/Scottish
Pet: A dachshund named Tobi Wan Kenobi
First Ambitions: To be an entertainer or a policeman
Musical instruments: Piano, saxophone
Cars: 1998 yellow SLK Mercedes and he has a BMW too

FAVORITES

Singer/Producer: Babyface
Musical Groups: Blackstreet, Boyz II Men
Song: All-4-One's "I Swear"
Actors: Samuel L. Jackson, Dustin Hoffman
Actress: Geena Davis
TV Shows: *Boy Meets World, Seinfeld*
Car: It used to be a Lexus, but now it's his new SLK Mercedes
Fast Food: McDonald's Double Cheeseburger
Breakfast: Eggs and bacon and toast
Ice Cream: Vanilla with caramel topping, and mint chocolate chip
Drinks: Mountain Dew and iced tea

Midnight Snack: Hershey's Cookies and Cream Chocolate bar

Candy: Jelly beans — especially yellow ones

Snack: Tostidos

Colors: Yellow, and sometimes purple

Clothes: Baggy style; designers Tommy Hilfiger, CK, DKNY, F8. And a new label called Dada — "The company's owned by a guy who's my age, he's just nineteen," A.J. told *Smash Hits*.

School Subjects: English, history (math is his least favorite)

Sports: Billiards, basketball, volleyball

Pastimes: Going to the movies, clubbing, shopping

Hobbies: Drawing cartoons, puppeteering

Video Game: Mortal Kombat

Cologne: CK One

Deodorant: Gillette

Saying: "It's gonna be funky!"

UP-CLOSE-AND-PERSONAL

Biggest Dislike: Two-faced people

One Wish: "To be in this business my whole life and live happily ever after."

Most Prized Possession: "My class ring."

Self-Description: "Crazy, cool, fun, big-hearted, outgoing."

If He Could Change One Thing About Himself: "My nose!"

Historical Era He Would Like to Visit: "Medieval times because of the clothing."

Something New He'd Like to Try: Skydiving

Dream Girl: "Someone who can be humorous as well as serious, honest, open-minded, respectful."

Dream Date: "Anywhere the lady would like, doing anything the lady would like."

Surprise Talent: He's a ventriloquist

Secret Passions: He loves to write poetry and read Shakespeare.

Collections: Hats and sunglasses

Secret Crushes: Alicia Silverstone and Liv Tyler

Hair Scares: A.J. has brown hair, but it once turned blond because of a chemistry experiment with Nick; he's also shaved his head!

First Time on Stage: A school production of *Snow White and the Seven Dwarfs* — he played Dopey!

Secret Facts: He's *not* good at keeping secrets and loves to make phone calls — anywhere, anytime!

Secret Prized Possession: "I had this blanket — 'my blankie' — that my great-grandmother knitted for me," he told *BIG!* magazine. "But I left it in a hotel room and I really miss it. That's why I twirl my clothes — it's what I used to do to my blankie. The trouble is now my clothes have holes all over them!"

Biggest Influence: An uncle who was in an early

rock band called Richie and the Rockets — "He was a big influence on me even though they never made it big," A.J. told a British reporter.

What People Would Be Surprised To Know: "I love Jackie Chan movies — I've seen all of them!" A.J. revealed in an online chat.

Known As: The group's flirt!

KEVIN SCOTT RICHARDSON

Nicknames: Mr. Body Beautiful, Kev, Boo, Kevi, Train

Birth Date: October 3, 1972

Zodiac Sign: Libra

Birth Place: Lexington, Kentucky

Current Residence: Orlando, Florida

Weight: 175 pounds

Height: 6'1"

Hair: Dark brown

Eyes: Green

Parents: Ann and Jerald Richardson Sr.

Siblings: Brothers Jerald and Tim

Most Famous Cousin: Brian Littrell

Pet: Cat named Quincy

First Ambitions: To be a singer and to be a pilot

Musical Instrument: Piano

FAVORITES

Book: *Interview With a Vampire* by Anne Rice

Singers: D'Angelo, The Artist (Formerly Known as Prince), Elton John, Billy Joel

Musical Idol: Elton John

Musical Group: The Eagles

Song: New Edition's "Hit Me Off"

Movie: *The Shawshank Redemption*

TV Shows: *Martin, Roseanne*

Actors: Tom Hanks, Robert DeNiro, John Travolta, Tom Cruise

Actresses: Nicole Kidman, Demi Moore, Michelle Pfeiffer

Food: "My mom's cooking!" Also Mexican and Chinese

Snack: "Peanut butter and jam on Ritz crackers — I could eat those babies all day!"

Breakfast: Waffles or pancakes with maple syrup

Ice Cream: Ben&Jerry's Peanut Butter and chocolate

Colors: Black, blue

Car: BMW 850

Cologne: XS de Paco Rabanne

School Subjects: History, geometry (least favorite — algebra)

Sports: Football, surfing, rugby, horseback riding, swimming

Pastimes: Watching films, weightlifting

Childhood Memory: Christmastime

Getaway Place: "Home to my family in Kentucky."

Hobby: Dancing, shooting hoops

Jewelry: Rings

Saying: "What's up?"

UP-CLOSE-AND-PERSONAL

Dream Girl: "Honest, with a nice smile and style."

Dream Date: Dinner, a movie, dancing

Major Turnoff: Racism and arrogant people

One Wish: "To see my father again — he died in 1991."

Self-Description: "Honest, sincere, and dedicated," and "I'm a shy guy," he told *BOP!* "Sometimes I think too much about what I'm going to say to somebody or what they are going to think."

Recent Vehicle Purchase: Black Toyota 4-Runner Limited

Historical Era He Would Like to Visit: "Medieval times — knights and castles — cool! Also the 1960s."

Something New He Would Like to Try: Skydiving

Surprise Fact: He used to work at Disney World as a tour guide, and as Aladdin and a Teenage Mutant Ninja Turtle in parades and shows.

If He Weren't in Show Biz: ". . . I'd be a teacher or a coach."

Secret Confession: "I wish I had A.J.'s voice — he has that raspy, soul-funk."

Major Crush: Liv Tyler

HOWARD DWAINE DOROUGH
Nicknames: Howie D., Sweet D, Latin Lover
Birth Date: August 22, 1973

Zodiac Sign: Leo
Birth Place: Orlando, Florida
Current Residence: Orlando, Florida
Weight: 135 pounds
Height: 5'6"
Hair: Brown
Eyes: Brown
Parents: Paula and Hoke Dorough
Siblings: John, Polly, Caroline, Angela —
Howie's the baby!
Heritage: Irish/Puerto Rican
Pet: Himalayan cat named Christopher and a
Pekingese dog named Oscar
First Ambition: To be a world-wide-known en-
tertainer
First Album Bought: Michael Jackson's *Thriller*
Musical Instruments: Piano and guitar
Cars: A Corvette and a truck

FAVORITES

Book: *The Firm* by John Grisham
Singers: Jon Secada, Al B. Sure, Phillip Bailey
Type of Music: Soul, R & B
Musical Group: Boyz II Men
Song: The Righteous Brothers "Unchained
Melody"
Movies: *The Outsiders, Willy Wonka and the
Chocolate Factory*
Actor: Tom Hanks
Actress: Demi Moore

TV Shows: Reruns of *Married . . . With Children* and *Fresh Prince of Bel Air* and *America's Funniest Home Videos*

Food: Chinese . . . but he confesses, "I love to cook and eat Indian food, even though my hamburger and fries are just awesome!"

Breakfast: Pancakes with maple syrup

Drinks: Sprite and iced tea

Ice Cream: Oreo Cookies and Cream

Colors: Purple

Car: Corvette

School Subject: Math (least favorite — English)

Clothes: Tommy Hilfiger

Cologne: CK One

Sports: Water sports like skiing and knee-skiing, racquetball

Pastimes: Acting, dancing, clubbing, going to the movies

Childhood Memory: "Spending Christmas with all my family."

Getaway Place: "To my family's house in Orlando or Puerto Rico."

Sports Team: Montreal Expos

Saying: "Cheers!"

UP-CLOSE-AND-PERSONAL

Dream Girl: "A girl who has a good head on her shoulders and knows what she wants in life."

Dream Date: "Going out for a candlelit dinner,

then to the movies, out dancing, and finally out to walk on the beach at night."

Major Turnoff: Selfish people, racism, prejudice

Self-Description: "I'm an honest, sincere person who cares a lot about other people and their feelings."

Best Quality: "Being a perfectionist."

Worst Quality: "Being a perfectionist . . . and sleeping late!"

Historical Era He Would Like to Visit: "The 1950s because I love the style of music and living back then."

If I Were an Inanimate Object: "I would be a car because I like living in the fast lane."

Who He Would Like to Ask Out to Dinner: Cindy Crawford

What He Brings on the Road: "My book bag, which has my whole house in it! CD player, CDs, cassette player, Spanish books, sunglasses — I have just about everything and anything!" He also brings a pocket-sized tape recorder and records his thoughts and observations.

Most Prized Possession: "My family and my career."

Secret Confession: He sleeps in his underwear!

Secret Disguise: A baseball cap

Secret Habit: He snores!

Secret Dream: To cruise around the Caribbean in a sailboat!

Little Known Facts: He was in one of the last classroom scenes of the movie *Parenthood* and starred in the pilot of Nickelodeon's *Welcome Freshman*.

Known As: The group's peacemaker

Secret Desire: "I'm in the process of growing my hair long — I want it past my shoulders," he told *Smash Hits*.

BRIAN THOMAS LITTRELL

Nicknames: B-Rok, Seaver, Mr. Joker, B

Birth Date: February 20, 1975

Zodiac Sign: Pisces

Birth Place: Lexington, Kentucky

Current Residence: Orlando, Florida

Weight: 135 pounds

Height: 5'7"

Hair: Dirty blond

Eyes: Blue

Parents: Harold and Jackie Littrell

Siblings: Older brother Harold

Most Famous Cousin: Kevin Richardson

Pet: A cat named Missy

First Ambitions: Singing and sports

Musical Instrument: Trumpet

High School: Tates Creek High School

Car: Jeep

FAVORITES

Singer/Producer: Babyface
Musical Groups: Boyz II Men, Jodeci
Singer: Luther Vandross
Song: "Too many to name"
Movie: *Star Wars* and almost any Jim Carrey movie
Actors: Tom Hanks, Jim Carrey
Actresses: Sandra Bullock, Whoopi Goldberg, Demi Moore
TV Shows: *Friends,* reruns of *Fresh Prince of Bel Air*
Foods: Pizza, macaroni and cheese
Breakfast: Frosted Flakes, toast with strawberry jam, and orange juice
Ice Cream: Plain vanilla with chocolate chips
Drink: Ginger ale and iced tea
Colors: Midnight blue
Car: Mercedes Benz
School Subject: Math (least favorite — English)
Sports: Basketball, golf, swimming
Pastimes: Going to the movies, listening to music
Hobbies: Weight lifting
Getaway Place: Home
Colognes: Photo de Lagerfeld and Safari
Clothes: Tommy Hilfiger

UP-CLOSE-AND-PERSONAL

Dream Girl: "A girl who is herself."
Dream Date: "Getting to really know someone."

Fantasy Girl: Pamela Anderson Lee

Major Turnoff: Racism

Self-Description: "Crazy, funny — what else can I say?"

If I Were an Inanimate Object: "A basketball."

Most Prized Possession: "My car, right now."

Surprise Possession: A king-sized water bed he bought for $50!

If He Weren't In Show Biz . . . : "I'd be in college — I was offered a singing scholarship to the University of Cincinnati Bible College."

What He Misses Most: "Having freedom."

Worst Fear: High places

Secret Confession: "I bite my fingernails — I've tried to stop but I can't. It bothers me because when I'm signing autographs, the girls are like, 'You bite your nails!'"

Secret Desire: "I'm seriously thinking about getting a tattoo," Brian told *Smash Hits*.

Known As: The group's funny man

Always Brings on Tour: A basketball

10
Backstreet Boys Discography

"I was in my Jeep at home, and I turned on the radio and heard a mix of 'Quit Playing Games' I never heard before. It still takes us by surprise. It was a really cool mix and I got cold chills! It's like no matter how many times I've heard it, it doesn't get old!"
— *Brian Littrell* **(Teen Beat)**

U.K. Albums
Backstreet Boys — 1996
"We've Got It Goin' On"
"Anywhere for You"
"Get Down (You're the One for Me)"
"I'll Never Break Your Heart"
"Quit Playing Games (With My Heart)"
"Boys Will Be Boys"
"Just to Be Close to You"
"I Wanna Be With You"

"Every Time I Close My Eyes"
"Darlin'"
"Let's Have a Party"
"Roll With It"
"Nobody But You"

Backstreet's Back — 1997
"Everybody (Backstreet's Back)"
"As Long As You Love Me"
"All I Have to Give"
"That's the Way I Like It"
"10,000 Promises"
"Like a Child"
"Hey, Mr. DJ (Keep Playin' This Song)"
"Set Adrift on Memory Bliss"
"That's What She Said"
"Anywhere for You"
"If You Want It to Be Good Girl (Get Yourself a
    Bad Boy)"
"If I Don't Have You"

UK / European / Canadian Single Releases
"We've Got It Goin' On"
"Get Down"
"I'll Never Break Your Heart"
"Quit Playing Games (With My Heart)"
"Anywhere for You"
"Nobody but You"
"Give Me Your Heart"
"Christmas Time"

"Lay Down Beside Me"
"Donde Quieras Yo Ire" ("Anywhere for You" in
 Spanish)

U.S. Albums
Backstreet Boys — 1997
"We've Got It Goin' On"
"Quit Playing Games (With My Heart)"
"As Long As You Love Me"
"All I Have to Give"
"Anywhere for You"
"Hey, Mr. DJ (Keep Playin' This Song)"
"I'll Never Break Your Heart"
"Darlin'"
"Get Down (You're the One for Me)"
"Set Adrift on Memory Bliss"
"If You Want It to Be Good Girl (Get Yourself a
 Bad Boy)"

Backstreet Boys — 1997 Enhanced CD*
"We've Got It Goin' On"
"Quit Playing Games (With My Heart)"
"As Long As You Love Me"
"Everybody (Backstreet's Back)" *Extended Ver-
 sion*
"All I Have to Give"
"Anywhere for You"
"Hey, Mr. DJ (Keep Playin' This Song)"
"I'll Never Break Your Heart"
"Darlin'"

"Get Down (You're the One for Me)"
"Set Adrift on Memory Bliss"
"If You Want It to Be Good Girl (Get Yourself a
   Bad Boy)"

* An enhanced CD is a regular audio CD with a multimedia CD-ROM track. With this enhanced CD you get a choice of four areas to explore: Biographies (which have info on the history of the group as well as individual bios complete with audio of the Boys); Hangin' With the Boys (which includes quick time videos of the Boys talking about things like their favorite food, their idea of a perfect date, funny things that happened to them on tour, and lots more!); Cool Stuff (which gives you info on available BSB merchandise); and Videos (which give you quick time videos — emphasis on the word *quick* — of two BSB videos, *Quit Playing Games (With My Heart)* and *We've Got It Goin' On*).

U.S. Singles
"We've Got It Goin' On"
"Quit Playing Games (With My Heart)"
"As Long As You Love Me"
"Everybody (Backstreet's Back)"
"All I Have to Give"

Videos
"We've Got It Goin' On"
"Quit Playing Games (With My Heart)"
"As Long As You Love Me"
"All I Have to Give"

Backstreet Boys: The Video (released in Europe)
"We've Got It Goin' On"
"Anywhere for You"
"I'll Never Break Your Heart"
"Get Down (You're the One for Me)"
"Quit Playing Games (With My Heart)"

Backstreet Boys Live in Concert Video (released in Europe)
"Let's Have a Party"
"End of the Road"
"Just to Be Close"
"I'll Never Break Your Heart"
"Ain't Nobody" (Instrumental)
"I Wanna Be With You"
"Anywhere for You"
"Darlin'"
"10,000 Promises"
"Boys Will Be Boys"
"Get Down (You're the One for Me)"
"Quit Playing Games (With My Heart)"

11
Tons of Trivia

"Being real. That's what makes us special . . .
being real.
We have nothing to hide."
— *A.J. McLean* (Teen Beat)

Even the most die-hard Backstreet Boys' fan can learn something new! Check out the following trivia tidbits and test your BSB-IQ!

1. When a Scholastic magazines writer asked A.J. if there was anything he would change about himself, he said: "My nose! Growing up as a kid, a lot of kids made fun of my nose and said it was big. But I guess that's where I get my soulful voice. . . . And my weight — I'm not exactly the biggest person in the world. I've got a good body, not to be conceited. I'm built well, but I'm kind of skinny."
2. Kevin told *Entertainment Weekly* that he was

a bit worried about all the stuff that goes along with success. "TV cartoons, bed sheets, dolls . . . I don't know all about that. There is such a thing as oversaturation." One thing Kevin is definitely not turning down is the Backstreet Boys comic book — created and designed by none other than fellow BSB, Nick Carter! The storyline, Nick told *Entertainment Weekly*, involves "each of us developing a power, like mutants, and battling a group of aliens who are trying to take over the world through music."

3. According to *TV Hits* magazine, the first thing A.J. asked to see when they visited an Australian wildlife park was a "Tasmanian tiger!" When he was told they were extinct, he realized he meant a Tasmanian devil — like in the cartoons. But when the park guide told him they were ferocious, he gave up the idea of holding one!

4. As a little kid Kevin says he loved Dr. Seuss' *The Cat in the Hat* book. He developed such a love of reading from the Seuss series, he told *BOP!*, "I always take books to read [when I go on tour]."

5. Nick used to baby-sit his young brother and sisters! "It was always a lot of fun because I really love my brother and sisters," he told *BOP!*

6. Kevin asked singer Bryan Adams for his autograph when they met at Britain's *Top of the Pops* show.

7. Kevin's father ran a summer camp back home in Kentucky and, as a kid, Kev used to help out cleaning cabins and cutting the grass!

8. A.J. once competed against Howie in a talent show — and beat him! "I won a thousand dollars," he told *Live & Kicking*. "It was the very first time I met Howie."

9. Mr. Romance, Brian, recalls he once had a crush on a girl at school. "I knew the combination to her locker, so I smuggled a dozen red roses into it to surprise her," he told *Live & Kicking*. "It sure did the trick!"

10. Brian told *BIG!* he would like to look like: "Brad Pitt — he's really good-looking and all the girls go for him. I'd like to look like Tom Cruise, too. Some people have said I look like him. Unfortunately, I don't anymore, because I've just dyed my hair red. I had a sudden urge to go a deep, dark red color. I like it a lot."

11. Howie is a big experimenter. "I'm a real adventurer when it comes to food," Howie told *BOP!* "So in every country I try to eat something that was a tradition of that country. Like in Ireland, I had fish and chips, and in England, since they have a lot of people from India living there, I had some Indian food, like curry."

12. When BSB was over in Belgium recently, they told *Live & Kicking* about one of the best perks they ever received — they got five Honda scooters. "These are the coolest freebies we've ever been given," Howie gushed. "We had the day off yesterday and took them to the local race track to test them out." Nick was thrilled with his scooter, too, and said, "I've wanted a scooter ever since Liam Gallagher [of Oasis] was given one of those really cool, slinky Lambrettas. I can't wait to get back on it, hit the road, and feel wind in my hair. It'll be cool!"

13. Backstage at a concert, the boys like to have certain snacks — a vegetable platter with dip, cheese and crackers, apples, oranges, lemons, orange juice, bottled water, Coca-Cola, Orange Crush, and Grape Crush.

14. Because their onstage choreography is so demanding, all of the boys have been known to lose up to four-and-a-half pounds each a performance!

15. Jive Records gave each of the boys a cellular phone so they can be in touch with their families no matter where they are!

16. Early in 1997, BSB appeared in Montreal and A.J. sprained his ankle as the group made a getaway from 10,000 screaming fans! But that didn't stop him from performing. He got right back on stage and danced away — soft cast and all. By the way (according to *USA Today*) the cast was auctioned off by a Canadian radio station!

17. BSB are ambassadors for SADD — Students Against Drunk Driving.

18. Brian and A.J. share an apartment in Orlando; Howie moved back to his family's home; Nick lives at home, too; and Kevin is moving into a place of his own.

19. The Backstreet Boys choreographer is Tina Robinson — she's worked with Michael Jackson, Brandy, and Bobby Brown.

Backstreet Boys Spill the Beans on Each Other!

According to BB magazine . . .

Nick: "Brian is basically a nut! He's very, very, very, very funny — off the wall!"

Brian: "Nick is very goofy. We probably get along the best out of everybody."

Howie: "[A.J. and I] crack on each other all the time."

A.J.: "[Howie and I] are on each other all the time. But we don't take it personally. There'll be times when it goes a little too far, and we get personal and then we go, 'All right, that's enough.' But if it's just joking, we just go off."

From an Online interview . . .

Kevin: "Nick is young and he has enormous energy. I would like to be so nonchalant and free as he is. He doesn't want anything serious — perhaps because he's only seventeen years old. . . . He is, definitely, the most clumsy of the group, but it is only because he has been growing [a lot]."

Brian: "Nick is like my younger brother that I never had. I can teach and help him to do many things. He doesn't love to lose in sports, and always gets mad when I beat him in Nintendo games. But he is a considerably mature man for his seventeen years."

Howie: "Brian is the person who draws attention nonstop. A.J., let's say, starts a story, but nobody listens to him, and we all look at Brian, who makes totally silly faces!"

Howie: "Kevin is a mature man, responsible, proficient, and knows exactly what he wants. He is a natural leader and keeps us together."

Nick: "Howie has a really twisted wardrobe. A few years ago, he constantly wore narrow pants, while the whole world wore wide. Now it's more modern to wear narrow pants, and he walks in wide pants. But that's Howie."

In a *Smash Hits* article . . .

Brian: "Howie is the peacemaker of the group. Nick's nickname is Chaos — he's just out of control. A.J. is Mr. Talkative and Kevin is Mr. Big Brother. I'm the comedian."

Nick: "A.J. — different. Brian — funny. Kevin — sophisticated. Howie — unpredictable. Myself — I don't know. I just try to be myself."

Kevin: "Howie's very laid-back — he's probably

the easiest going of the group. Me, I'm a perfectionist — I want things just right. We have rows sometimes because of that. Brian — jokester, likes to play around, but he's got a serious side as well. We've all got a serious side; you've gotta make time to be serious about what you're doing. A.J. is very laid-back as well . . . [he] talks a lot, especially with girls!"

Howie: "I'm called Sweet-D — I'm sweet with the ladies, I guess. Brian is, of course, known as B-Rok for his basketball playing. A.J. is the skinny one. Kevin is the most focused. I call Nick and Brian 'Frick and Frack' as they're really such a double act when they're together."

A.J.: "Brian's the clown. Howie's really sweet, kinda like a suave character. Kevin is very professional and serious, yet with a very sensitive side. And me? Just crazy!"

TV Hits **magazine asked the boys questions about each other and they had some telling answers. . . .**

How's Brian coping with fame?

Nick: "Really well. He's totally stayed the same. I think we're all coping well, to be honest. I don't think it's affected him at all, but you'll have to come back and check with me in a few years, then I'll be able to tell you if he's changed or not!"

What will Nick buy with his first million dollars?

Brian: "A whole heap of video games, that's for sure! First he'd pay off his parents' house for them. It's a really nice home and he's told me he wants to stay there until he's at least twenty, when he gets his own place. Then he'd go out and buy a lot of video games and a really cool entertainment system."

And, finally, in an interview with a Scholastic magazines writer . . .

Howie: "A.J. is definitely the most flirtatious communicator. Brian is the comedian. Nick is full of energy. Kevin is the more serious side of BSB and I am the peacemaker — at least that's what they call me."

12
How to Make
the BSB Connection

**"This is our dream. We wanted
to make it happen and that's what we did. And we
are enjoying every moment of it. . . ."
— *Nick Carter* (Teen Beat)**

So you want to get in touch with Nick, Kevin, A.J., Howie, and Brian? That's easy, just let your fingers do the walking — by letter, online, or even phone!

THE U.S.A. BACKSTREET BOYS FAN CLUB
P.O. Box 618203
Orlando, Florida 32861-8203

THE CANADIAN BACKSTREET BOYS FAN CLUB

Romper Holdings Limited
Fan Club Suite 1231
1930 Yonge Street
Toronto, Ontario M4S 1Z7

THE HOLLAND BACKSTREET BOYS FAN CLUB

P.O. Box 713
4116ZJ Buren [Gld]
The Netherlands

BACKSTREET BOYS OFFICIAL ONLINE ADDRESS:

http://www.backstreetboys.com

JIVE RECORDS

c/o Backstreet Boys
137-139 West 25th Street
New York, NY 10001

BACKSTREET BOYS ANSWERING MACHINES:

1 (407) 880-7000 (there is a long distance charge; be sure to get a parent's permission!)

1 (888) 344-7717 (this is a free call in the U.S.)

WOULD YOU BELIEVE IT IF SOMEONE TOLD YOU...

"Never told before" stories

Leonardo DiCaprio was a terrible student?

Will Smith and his parents battled over his decision not to go to college?

Michelle Williams was the total opposite of the cool and popular "Jen" she plays on *Dawson's Creek?*

WHAT IF <u>THEY</u> TOLD YOU?

These celebrities and others—including Hanson, Jewel, The Backstreet Boys, and the casts of *Party of Five* and *Buffy the Vampire Slayer*—tell you all the secrets you never knew, and how their experiences made them who they are today.

GOT ISSUES MUCH?
Celebrities Share Their Traumas and Triumphs

In bookstores December 1998!